BROKEN

Ta'Quell Morris-Rodriguez

Publishing Services by Stanton Publishing House

Library of Congress Registration Number: 2020912078

ISBN: 9798640383119 (KDP Amazon Paperback)

ISBN: 9781663524454 (Barnes & Noble Paperback)

Printed in the United States of America

Acknowledgments

Book Cover Design & Graphics: Tru Soundz

Foreword: Mrs. Ellen Eagen

Thank you to my son Davion and my bonus sons Keno & Khamari (Foster sons).

Thank you to my siblings Glady, Jeremiah & Daniel.

Thank you to my step-father, Ralph Young.

A huge thank you to my Family (Curtis, Shaka, Siera, Alex, Julian, Anthony, Joe, Houston, Toya & Doryen) without you all boy oh boy I would be messed up somewhere for real.

Finally, thank you so much to everyone that taught me how to manage life while I was at the bottom because now I am loving how great it feels to live up here.

Table of Contents

FOREWORD

When I first met Ta'Quell Morris, I saw a tall, stately, and thoughtful educator who was curious to learn about our new, innovative high school in Syracuse, New York. Only months later when I interviewed Ta'Quell for the position of dean did he tell me that he was the young man whose family did not come to see his 8th grade graduation. And, you can imagine my surprise, when Ta'Quell, now Head of Community and Culture at our high school, introduced himself to our school's impartial hearing officer as the young man who this same impartial hearing officer had expelled from school 17 years earlier. You don't see that Ta'Quell now but Broken paints the portrait of a sad and neglected young boy acting out against the abuse and abandonment life had dished out to him. With each chapter of <u>Broken</u>, you feel one bandage ripped off after the other.

What is so amazing about Ta'Quell's story is that there are no wounds to be seen now. As I am writing this during a Christmas holiday, Ta'Quell is sitting at his oldest son's bedside at Upstate Golisano Children's Hospital, and we are having a text discussion about the little boy's breakfast nutrition. In chapter 7 Ta'Quell mentions his son, Davion. But the story continues. Several weeks ago, Ta'Quell became the single-parent of three little boys. Ta'Quell not only regained sole custody of his own son, Davion, who is now 4 years old, but he was asked by the court to foster Davion's siblings, a one-year old and an eight-year-old. Their mom remains part of the pattern of abuse and sadness that Ta'Quell grapples with so compassionately in his memoir. So, this is how the story goes: the young man who shares with us his story of the painful absence of a father figure becomes the father and not just any father—the father who cooks, cleans, decorates the home for Christmas, goes to their school regularly, knows his boys' shirt sizes and sits by their bedside when they are sick. True it is a story about being broken, but it is much more a story about healing—reminding me of Alice Walker's quotation "healing begins where the wound is made."

I must admit it is hard to read this story—as a parent, as an educator, as a lawyer, as a colleague, as a friend—not only because it is Ta'Quell's personal journey but because I know it is not only his story, but it is the story of so many of our students. Yet, the amazing part of this is Ta'Quell's ability to survive with such grace. Some might call this a miracle. But, I think that the answer is more tangible. What Ta'Quell has is a mix of passion and perseverance—what the renown twenty-first century neuroscientist, Angela Duckworth calls, "grit." This is what sets Ta'Quell Morris apart from others—this is the edge that is inherent in the children from our community, that if harnessed is the super-power that can break the chains of any dysfunctional environment.

In Broken Ta'Quell Morris tells us how he heals and thrives. The good news is that there are "Ta'Quells" across the cities and towns of our country—young men and women who grow up to overcome the disadvantages of their youth, who harness the spirit and love of their aunts, grandmothers, pastors, and then begin to heal, leading the way to help others to do the same—this is an act to celebrate, a book to celebrate. Congratulations, Ta'Quell. I am confident Gramz is looking down on you and is very proud.

With admiration,

Ellen Eagen

Eagen Law Firm LLC, Education Lawyer/Lecturer in Law & Writing Instructor at Stanford Law School

December 2019

.

DEDICATIONS

This book is dedicated to the three most important people in my life, my Gramz (Bobbie Mae Kaigler), my father Sylvio Rodriguez & my mother Stacy Rodriguez (Young). Without the three of you, there would be no me, and I wouldn't even know how to handle the thorns in life I've been handed.

Additionally, to every person that picks up this book that has endured any type of pain, hardships, frustration, and hurt; this book is dedicated to you as well. To the individual that may not feel they are worth it, you can make it, ask me how I know.

INTRODUCTION

Some books often are positioned soundlessly in the corner of your mind until it's time to dispense the kaput product before your audience. Some books need to be coaxed onto the paper. Meanwhile, there are still other books that plead to be printed, with an earnestness unable to be muzzled. Sentences may hurdle with recklessness. This is one of those books for sure.

I want to share a story with you. It's a tough story, but one I need to communicate. It's about being broken. Broken, yet……

Maybe you are broken, and perchance you do not even know that you are broken. We're not complete, life indeed is a process, some days good and others well....

If we are honest some would say Life is hard, wouldn't you agree? Some things I anticipated would happen in my life, unfortunately, didn't; while other things I never imagined, emerged before my wide-open eyes.

Life doesn't end with brokenness; that's where it begins. If I may perhaps share a message; it would simply be frequently kids who go through trauma whether it be loss, abuse, or neglect are often misinterpreted whether it's in schools and/or just everyday life. Typically, these are those kids who will most likely not perform well, behave rebelliously, and sometimes just don't fit in. For one reason or another, this represents our schools in that they are typically set up to best benefit children from supportive homes, who frequently display good behavior.

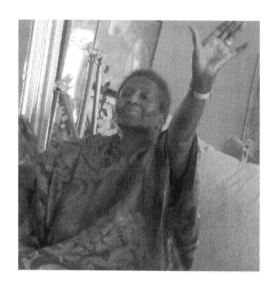

CHAPTER 1: "CALLED"

Many would read the title of a book called "Broken" and think to themselves, not another autobiography. Do I really care to know or hear another life story? With that being said, I can honestly say that I wish I had a "me" in my life as a child to serve as a mentor and a guiding light. Just for a moment, I'd like for you to empathize and completely place yourself in the shoes of a young man, that grew up on the south side of Syracuse NY in the "Hood." With a father that sold drugs and a mother who smoked them, I was a kid that felt alone more often than ever.

"For many are called, but few are chosen."

~Matthew 22:14 (KJV)

At the early age of five years old, I can remember spending most of my time at my grandmother's house. I preferred to call it Gramz house. I have very fond memories of that time in my life and as I think back I can hear the fish grease popping. I can vividly see Gramz wearing her dashiki dress in the kitchen while frying multiple pieces of fish for her grandkids.

Spending time at Gramz house was the most fun I ever had. The brown and white three-bedroom home sat on the South Side of Syracuse, and the closed-in porch is where we would jump over the rails playing with each other and neighborhood friends. I'll never forget the sound of the stairs squeaking. Because even when no one was walking on them they still managed to squeak and those sounds still play vividly in my mind.

Summers at Gramz house were totally different from summers at home with my mother because my Gramz was a God-fearing Apostolic woman that didn't play about her religion and she represented what most would refer to as a holy roller. And to be honest she proudly represented. Gramz wasn't the type to lie no matter what the benefit was because she wouldn't even allow us to use her address so that we could attend the summer recreation center in her neighborhood. She refused to do wrong promising that wrong would always catch up to us.

Spending the entire summer at Gramz house wasn't that bad because Gramz was always cooking up something in the kitchen. My favorite was her famous fried salmon patties with white rice, complemented by an ice-cold Pepsi on the side. I can taste it right now just thinking about it. Most summer days my friends would be outside playing with each other. We did it all from wrestling, playing hopscotch, race, tag, hot potato, and even playing house.

After spending most of my time playing outside I would hear my grandmother's raspy voice yelling from the cracked screen door "TA'QUELL" once the sun began to set. Whenever she called me I knew that meant that it was time for me to come in. Even though it was still light outside and the street lights hadn't come on it was best for me to head on inside.

Once I got in the house she would say,

"Baby, do you need to eat a little bit? We got to be to church in an hour."

As a kid, I hated church because we were in church literally six days a week and never failed to miss a service. I just wanted to be a kid, hang with my friends, and run up and down the streets in the hood. I didn't think that I was asking for much but apparently, I was. So, the potholes, the dogs in just about in every yard, and my most trusted friends would have to wait while I was forced to go to church.

We had a bible study on Tuesday, some sort of service on Wednesday night. Then, Thursday evangelistic night service, and on Friday my Gramz always had to be at the church for something. On Saturday's we had prayer and choir rehearsal and then all-day Sunday we had church. Sunday school started promptly at 9:45 and we still didn't get out of service until 230 or 3:00 pm. The night service began at 7 pm and didn't end until around 10 pm.

I felt my resentment for church growing early and being forced to attend church multiple days a week while never experiencing the entire purpose of church left me somewhat lost. I can honestly say that

I learned about God, but I didn't learn how to seek him out and find him for myself. I knew all the bible stories, but I never learned how to relate the bible to my everyday life.

Now that I am grown, I do appreciate my Gramz for raising me in the church,

"Train up a child in the way they should go, and they will never depart from it"

~ Proverbs 22:6 (KIV)

Trust me I get it. At times you may think that you are wasting your time, or feel that things aren't working for you, you may even think that what you're doing doesn't make sense. But can I just reaffirm to you that God has not forgotten about you, your child, your nephew, your niece, etc., He is not a man that lies. One thing to remember is that God's timing is much different than ours and he is sure to never be late.

I knew at an early age that there was something a little different about my life compared to the lives of my friends and family, and frankly, it was a hard thing to comprehend. Most of the children my age lived in a family structure where their parents weren't saved and didn't go to church. They typically enjoyed their lives going to friends' houses and playing outside with other children their age; and meanwhile, I was either at church or getting ready for church.

Attending grade school was a terrible experience for me. I was different, I was a church boy, and I didn't fit in with the rest of the kids. I resented school daily all because I was somewhat of an outcast. I especially hated Halloween time. Most times I wasn't even allowed to attend school on this holiday. Not to mention that the church I attended as a child had long ago condemned Halloween as a holiday. They said it was celebrating devil worship.

Whenever I got lucky and was allowed to attend, I'd be the only child walking around angry because I didn't have a costume. This only contributed to my feelings of being an outcast and that I truly didn't belong. The Sense of not belonging was one of the worst feelings I had ever felt. Being an outcast finally started to settle as I would be amongst other children and start to feel as if I were alone regardless of how many other children were surrounding me.

Some say raising a child this way is right, and others will say raising a child that way is wrong. Honestly, I don't have the answers, but I can tell you in good faith that I know I am who I am today because of the training I had as a child. It wasn't until I became a teenager that my Bishop and I would have a more in-depth conversation. During one of our talks, he shared with me that I've never forgotten.

"Quell, some of the things that I learned in the church may not be a sin, but what I do know is that you will definitely make it to heaven this way." He said to me with a stern face.

When we finished that conversation my level of respect for him grew tremendously because I could finally relate to what he was saying after all this time. He pretty much told me that everything may not be in the bible, but he promised me that I would make it to heaven if I followed Christ.

How long

"So even if your life is full of people, if you don't regularly spend hours with a friend talking and listening about your concerns and hopes for life, if you don't take time to let your feet touch the earth, breathe in the fresh air in a beautiful environment, and fully feel gratitude and love throughout your body, your loneliness can be physically as well as mentally damaging." (Reynolds, 2013).

From a little child after having several pastors, prophets speaking over me that there was a great call on my life and on top of that I already knew that God had a plan for me; so with that, restrictions of living a set-apart lifestyle came along.

"Do not love the world [of sin that opposes God and His precepts], nor the things that are in the world. If anyone loves the world, the love of the father is not in him."

~ *1 John 2:15*

"But ye are a chosen generation, a royal priesthood, a holy nation, a peculiar people; that ye should shew forth the praises of him who hath called you out of darkness into his marvelous light."

~ *1 Peter 2:9*

As a young child, these scriptures meant nothing at all to me as I didn't understand what they meant all I knew was that I wanted to be normal and enjoy my childhood. I'm sure some of you can relate to being that child that had no freedom at all. My life was so restricted that it made me hate the fact that I was called and looked upon as a "church boy." As time passed by and I grew older my personal relationship with Jesus became stronger than ever as I had a yearning for God myself.

By the time I had made it to middle school, I can recall sitting around with friends talking about some movies they had gone to see with their family, friends, boyfriends, and girlfriends, etc. I always lied and acted as if I had seen the movie already with my imaginary girlfriend that never existed. I lied because the church that I grew up in didn't allow us to go to the movies. They said that "worldly" movies were a sin. (As much as I wanted to be normal this fed my sense of not belonging).

The 6th grade wasn't that bad at all come to think of it. And yes, I was a troubled child. I always slept in class, I was always in a fight, I argued with anyone that gave me problems, and I disrespected my teachers. Every time I turned around I was suspended from school. At one point, I got expelled from district school Grant Middle and had to attend Shea Middle school which wasn't too far away from our neighborhood.

Attending this school changed my life for the better because I became much more popular and I made plenty of friends at this school. This was the first time in years I was happy about being around people and I didn't feel alone and shamed.

One Thursday afternoon, when we were in the 3rd lunch period, my peers started singing

R&B music which the church referred to as secular music. Of course, the old church boy in me didn't know the words to the song but not knowing the words didn't stop me because I mumbled while everyone else sang along. It actually worked and made me not feel so bad because I hoped that people wouldn't realize how extremely hard I was trying to fit in. There are times when life will take us on one of its many diversions, and frequently leaves us feeling isolated. But, never give up. Sometimes the nature of life itself causes isolation.

Grasping the thought that our lives convey us to different intersections and that the deviations in our lives make it where we aren't able to be everywhere with others or at least not be around them comfortably. We oftentimes say God is perfect in all

15

his ways, and this is true. Especially when it comes to him blessing us with something we really deserve and desire, but when it comes to his selection of us, we seem to deem him unworthy of making the right decision.

CHAPTER 2: WONDERING WHAT THE DIFFERENCE IS?

"But you are the ones chosen by God, chosen for the high calling of priestly work, chosen to be a holy people, God's instruments to do his work and speak out for him."

~1 Peter 2:9

It was at an early age when I knew that I was different from everyone else. I can easily recall always being stressed out and often feeling depressed throughout my childhood. But I never really knew or had a full understanding as to why. I guess that I was just too young to understand what was going on with me at the time. There were times when things got rough for my family, and all I could think of were the times when church members would say: "God won't put more on you than you can bear." Although this scripture held true it had very little meaning to me back then. And I'm sure that's because I didn't really understand it. Being that I was still a young child my faith had not reached a level where I fully placed my trust in God.

But then there was that time when I felt the presence of God upon me. I'll never forget it because this was my first time ever having this kind of experience. I was in Utica, NY, it was on a Friday afternoon, and I was sitting in a church service at Greater Holy Temple Church over on Howard Avenue. The late elder Charles Stewart was officiating our choir rehearsal and workshop. I remember the whole thing clearly as if it happened yesterday. The choir was practicing and then Elder Stewart took his place in the middle of the room and began to minister just as he would normally do during rehearsals.

"When your back is up against the wall, God will hide you!"

The power of God shot through the pulpit and hit one of my friends. It must have bounced off her and fell on me; I will never forget it. I busted out into tears, my hands started to tremble, and the more I tried to control my body and stop the tears, the faster they fell from my cheeks. With the way, I cried out to God you would've thought that the main water line had broken somewhere nearby. My bottom lip started quivering as my arms flew up in the air, all before I could process what was happening. My tongue was moving on its own and then the words began to form and come forth. As the Church Folk say, I was speaking in tongues.

"And these signs will follow those who believe... they will speak with new tongues."

~ Mark 16:17

I was speaking a language that could only be understood if you were under the power of God. I did not understand what was happening, and I could not fathom what was going on. My leg shook uncontrollably, and before I knew it, I was shouting. It felt like something had taken over my entire body and with zero control of my body functions, I assumed that I had officially gone crazy. In fact, crazy enough to be admitted into a psychiatric ward. I was always that young person in the Holiness church that laughed and pointed at others when they were caught up in "the spirit." I always acted downright silly and a little disrespectful to others until it hit me. So, the first thing to come to mind was; here I am, after making fun of those people and I'm up here doing the same thing.

Today, I can look back and laugh because God wanted to show me that he is real and very well alive. By giving me the chance to experience him in full force. In the back of my mind, all I thought about was my friends and cousins that I often sat and joked with about catching the Holy Ghost. I knew they were laughing at me and that they would never let me live it down. I remember opening my eyes with feelings of shame and embarrassment only to see that my friends and cousins were crying and speaking in tongues too! That day I was completely blown away by the magnitude of God's power, and I was in awe of what we all experienced that night. The car ride home was completely silent the entire way from the church back to the Radisson Hotel. This ride seemed like the longest ride of my life. With millions of thoughts running through my head I tried to understand what had just taken place. "Oh, My Goodness did that really happen? Am I saved now? Do I have to act like the other "super holy" people? Will there have to be more restrictions on the way I act now?"

Getting out of the car and walking through the lobby of the hotel felt like I was in a Twilight zone it was as if time had frozen. My Gramz, my aunt, or my cousins were all left speechless and no one had said a thing about the rehearsal. That afternoon I tried to rest but I couldn't. All I kept thinking about was me actually speaking in tongues and having a one-on-one experience with my Lord and Savior Jesus Christ. Not to mention the fact that I was blown away by "God" choosing to talk to me. I wanted to talk to him too and let him know about all the time's people talked bad to me and had hurt my feelings. I also wanted him to know and about all the things that were going on in my home in addition to a ton of other things that were on my mind and my heart.

I couldn't wait for the next church service to take place. While getting dressed I kept thinking to myself "Oh boy, I can't wait to get to church and feel God again. I want to talk to him, I have so much to tell him, and it had been so long since I felt as happy as I did when his presence was upon me." I remember wearing a pair of brown khakis, and a tan sweater. Friday night services were always my favorite and now it was a great experience for me also because I was eager to commune with the father and feel his presence just as I did in the previous encounter. When the service started, the devotion leader was doing a great job getting the people stirred up and setting the tone for praise and worship. It was a lovely sight to see because they were giving God everything, they had in them. Personally, I didn't really care about the choir singing because I just wanted to feel Jesus again. Service that night seemed to drag on and on, and the passing of the offering plates seemed to take three weeks and a day! I was growing impatient and I could only anticipate my chance to speak with God again. I needed to tell him more about the things I had to endure in the first seven years of my life.

That night, the combined choir sang three different selections and they sang until just about everyone in the congregation was shouting except for me. They were falling out and talking in tongues while I felt nothing at all. The service progressed and my pastor, the late Bishop Alvin J. Nelson introduced Elder Stewart to the congregation halfway through the service. As the guest speaker, he began to minister under the unction of the Holy Spirit and while he ministered, I still felt absolutely nothing. Then during the altar call, which is a time for people who wanted to be saved and wanted prayer, I found myself in line. I was amongst one hundred or more people waiting to feel the presence of God again. And there was a part of me that was very angry that it was taking so long. Even though it was hard I knew I had to be patient.

When I finally made it to the front of the line to receive prayer and to feel the presence of God that I was desperately yearning, Elder Stewart told me to throw my gum out. I had waited in line for what felt like forever only to be turned away for chewing gum. I would've swallowed it, put it in my pocket without a wrapper, or even put it behind my ear for later if he had he given me the chance to. I couldn't understand what gum had to do with it because I just wanted to feel God's presence. I was angry because this was the same man who made me shout and feel God's presence earlier so why would he turn me away when all I wanted to do was feel connected to God again. I felt as if God no longer wanted to hear from me and the rejection hurt my feelings.

After all, my entire life I endured people walking in and walking out, so this didn't help one bit.

My mind flashed back to the age of seven when my house was raided. Our house had been raided several times before in the past, however, this time it was different. I can still hear my Dad screaming at the police officers. He only stood 5 feet and 4 inches tall, but he was all man and he demanded his respect

"Take your foot off of my furniture!" he yelled.

As the police searched for weapons and drugs. They flipped over couches, cut open the couch cushions, and knocked over tables. When I came out of my room to see what was happening, two officers were sticking their hands down inside of our fish tank, which was 300-gallon tank installed between the living room and dining room wall. I wasn't sure of what if anything they found, but I knew they took my father to jail. For years after that, I remember my mother and I getting on the bus to visit my father in prison. This lasted for seven of his ten-year sentence.

By the time my father was released, I had grown into a young adult. And to be honest I was excited but also reluctant to make a connection with him because I was afraid that he would leave me again and I was tired of feeling lost and alone. I had no one in my life on a consistent basis as we were always moving in and out of state. Sadly, I can't even remember anyone taking the time to tell me that they love me. I snapped out of my memories of my father and reminisced back on my encounter with God. I had never felt as loved and secure as I did with God at choir rehearsal. My emotions were all over the place and I began to regret my experience. I felt like God had abandoned me like everyone else and I didn't care anymore. As far as I was concerned, I was done with God.

And I'm sure that as you are reading my words, even you can admit there was a time that everything was not always "peachy" in your life. It's okay to be honest because we have all wanted to quit and give up at some point. I'm sure you wanted to give up on some family members, maybe your job, or your ministry, maybe even your church, sometimes your marriage and many of us won't admit it but there have even been times when we've wanted to quit and give up on God himself. But there was something in us that kept us holding on, with that little voice in the core of your gut saying, "I trust God too much to give up."

The next day was Saturday, and we spent most of the day rehearsing and preparing for a banquet that was planned in the main ballroom of the hotel where we were staying. The banquet was a great experience that we all enjoyed. There was plenty of food, fun, and laughter and I remember the choir singing "Melodies from Heaven." Surprisingly, I began to feel a tingling sensation in my stomach, but I tried to shake it off because I was still mad at God and Elder Stewart. I held back as long as I could but then the sermon preached that night was entitled "God I need more NOW." Before I knew it tears began to fall from my face instantly. It was as if the message was intended just for me and I began talking in tongues more than I had done previously and this time I already had the conversation in my head that I wanted to have with Jesus.

CHAPTER 3:
ANGRY &
BITTER

"In your anger do not sin. Do not let the sun go down while you are still angry, and do not give the devil a foothold."

~ Ephesians 4:26-27

Saturday there was a huge banquet at the church, and I wanted to personally tell God how angry I was about him ignoring me. I wanted to feel him and talk to him so badly, but he never answered me. Then I remember hearing my Gramz quote her favorite scripture. Every time she found herself frustrated; she would speak it. *"Deuteronomy 31:6, "I'll never leave you nor forsake you."*

I wanted God to know that I was angry and very bitter about having to visit my father in a prison because he was arrested for selling drugs. This was nearly my only memory of him and to this day I can still remember the police and the DT's kicking in our door and raiding our house, several times throughout the years. Whenever I close my eyes and think back, I hear the arguing and yelling between my parents during those days. I still hear the curse words; I still see dishes and other items flying through our house and the sound of them breaking once they made contact with the floor or wall. The doors slammed loudly and then the knock on the door from the police arriving once the fight was over.

In all honesty and fairness to my parents, as a child I had just about everything I ever wanted or could possibly think of except for friends. And then there was that genuine sense of love and the feeling of belonging to a group of people who truly cared for and loved me for me. I just wanted to be myself and I wanted true friends and family that weren't just around because of what my father could provide for them.

Alongside my father being in prison, my mother was pregnant again and was having a girl. I couldn't accurately process what was going on in my life at the time because everything that I had grown to know was changing so rapidly. At an early age I was more advanced than most, so it was easy for me to notice change. I've been frustrated at times with no one to talk to. Do you know the feeling? Maybe you had friends or family to vent to and share the things that were going on with you. Rest assured that there were times when I felt as if I was the only one going through and there are some people that will never ask you how you're doing. The funny thing is that when others have no concern for you somehow that's when you will find your strength, will, and resilience.

Resentment

As I continued to grow and learn times started getting very weird and difficult. My mother no longer kept her word as she had previously. She would drop us off with different family members and leave us for days at a time without even checking on us. This came as a shock and a surprise because my mom had always been a hands-on parent due to the fact that my father was in prison. My family members always spoke negative things about my mom and it would always hurt my feelings. I knew that my mother loved us regardless of what any of them said. At times I would not play with others and you would often find me alone to myself somewhere crying. I didn't want to be there with them, and I didn't want to hear anyone talking bad about my mom.

Being bounced around between different houses was hard, but at some point, I started to second guess whether my mother actually loved us or not. After hearing things like "she doesn't care about her kids, she just leaves her kids and won't even check on them. Stacy is so stupid and selfish!" All I ever heard was negative things in regard to my mother. Maybe some of you are able to relate to having a family system that says they love you but shows you something totally different through their actions.

I can remember sitting on the yellow porch in the neighborhood when I first heard someone say, "she's just a crack head, she needs to leave those drugs alone, her kids ain't never gonna be nothing because of her." As a kid it hurt to hear those words and they began to resonate in my heart that maybe my mom didn't love us. All this was around the same time that my cousin and aunt decided to blurt out that the man who I thought was my father actually wasn't. I was confused, upset, hurt, and broke after hearing the outburst. I didn't need to hear that I never asked them anything. So, for them to share that information it was done out of spite. I don't even understand why they felt like it was their place to do so anyway. With that being said I always say that people may have done you wrong but keep silent and watch God work."

Can anyone help me

Over time my mother started doing better when it came to getting her life together and her priorities in order. She was doing good for a while and life was in fact getting better. Then I came home from school one day and noticed that the things in our house were no longer there. When I asked my mom, what happened to our stuff she would constantly lie to me stating that someone broke in our house and stole our stuff. From then on, I watched the decline and my mother as she started to descend backward. She was using drugs more and every day more things came up missing.

If that wasn't enough, one Tuesday afternoon after my sister and I both arrived home from school after having a normal day. We ate our dinner and after a while it was night time, but our mom hadn't returned home as of yet. We had never stayed home by ourselves overnight before, so we were worried. I mean outside of her going out at night which was normal. We woke up the next morning and my mother still hadn't come home. I got up and made sure my sister made it to her bus stop by 6:20am and ran three blocks down the hill to catch the city bus by 6:40am in order for me to make it to school on time.

By the time we came home that day our mother was not at home and didn't return for several of days. I didn't dare tell my family members about it because whenever our mother would drop us off with them we would never hear the end of it. These instances helped form my sense of pride at a very early age. The first night she didn't come home I recall being very upset about it because I wondered what happened to her and where she was at. I didn't know what she was doing or if she was safe or even still alive. Growing up there were moments when all I could do was cry and hate God while blaming him for what he was allowing me to go through.

There were moments when it seemed like no one else could feel my pain or minister to the very need I had. Which was killing me on the inside. I had to learn how to keep myself together and how to smile while hurting on the inside. It started to become more evident when things were not going right around our home. I was the one running the house and I even had to go grocery shopping as a kid, as if I actually knew anything about shopping for food. But I was forced to learn. On top of having to go grocery shopping I had to remember my mother's food stamp card number so I could call and order a new card every month. I skipped school at the end of every month, so I could be home to get the card out of the mail. I had to be at the store on the first thing smoking or the food stamps would be gone before we knew it. I knew nothing about parenting or keeping a house at all, and to be honest I barely knew how to be a kid.

In all, the most hurtful thing was that no one saw through my lies about my mom being at work or sleep or not feeling well. I always covered for her and I just wish there would've been at least one person that would've just let me cry on their shoulder's because to be frankly honest I was completely exhausted, and overwhelmed. Often things in life happen and you don't understand at the moment why they're happening, but I understood, and I watched it all play out as clear as day.

At this point we were back living at our Gramz house and hadn't seen our mother in quite some time. I was riding down Midland Ave with my aunt on a Tuesday night after bible study and I saw my mother on the porch of a white and red house. I remember the screen door having a ton of holes in it when I screamed "Stop!" As my aunt slammed on the brakes I jumped out of the car so happy to see my mother. But I wasn't prepared for what was about to happen next.

I ran back the distance of a few houses and when I caught up to her she was so high that she didn't even know who I was. For the first couple minutes of talking I had to convince her that I was her son. When I got back in the maroon Taurus with my Aunt I tried to keep it together as if I was unbothered by the sight. But when my aunt said, "baby God's gonna fix it" I just broke down and I started screaming to the top of my lungs because I was so broken. I just wanted it all to stop. The pain, the resentment, and the anger, I just wanted God to take it all away.

I walked in Gramz house and took flight up the squeaky stairs and then I heard the phone ring. All I could hear was my Gramz scream "The Blood of Jesus!"

By this time, I'm in my room biting my pillow on the bottom bunk bed trying to muffle my screams and tears. My Gramz came up the stairs and sat on the bed next to me. She didn't say much other than "Ta'Quell the devil can't and won't stop you." She grabbed my hand and started praying for me. I remember her crying and saying God you got to save my baby, I plead the blood of Jesus over her life, and my baby shall be saved.

God is not slack

Sitting on the fourth row from the back of the church God told me when I was 12 years old that my mother would be saved. At the time I couldn't see how that was even possible looking through my natural eyes at the circumstances. But I held on to God's word in my heart and I began to pour blessed oil in my mother's shoes when she wasn't looking. I also anointed her pillows. It was not that I knew much about blessed oil, but my Bishop would use it every time he prayed for us, so I figured it would work. No, it didn't happen right away but if God says it whether I believe it or not that settles it. We can't be too concerned with the who, what, why, and where concerning God handling things. But needless to say, God definitely fulfilled his word and eventually saved my mother.

Times when I wanted to give up and quit, she ended up being there to push me and encourage me, so I would keep going. Some would ask how can you say all these negative things about your mom and then turn around and combat it with she's now saved. But I would like to say that nothing I share is to either demean or embarrass my mother, but my story is what made me who I am today. I wouldn't trade it for anything. For several years I lied about my past and who my parents were because I was ashamed and never wanted anyone to know that my father was in prison and my mother had a drug addiction. With them both being in and out of jail for years I was too embarrassed to say that they were my parents, and I didn't want to deal with everyone constantly asking me questions about them. I was nervous that some of my friends' families wouldn't want their child hanging around with me if they knew who my parents actually were.

If you are going through a difficult time, let this word bring you encouragement. God wants to give you double for your trouble and he is surely a God of restoration that means He's not going to just repay you for every wrong done but He's going to go above and beyond and make things much better than they ever were before. If you are facing challenges today or going through a time of adversity, remember it's always darkest just before dawn. Your days are destined to shine brighter because God is true and faithful. As you stand in your faith and you are obedient to His Word and His will, you'll receive double for your trouble and see His promises for your life come to pass!

BROKEN

I was once there, and I know that feeling oh too well. I would like to pray with you:

Father God, I thank You for Your Word which lights our path and guides our steps. God, I chose to put my trust and hope in You and through this reading, I pray the reader has enough strength to do the same. Thank You Father, for bringing restoration into my life and the life of anyone reading these words. As we keep our heart and mind stayed on You. In Jesus' Name we pray.

Amen

CHAPTER: 4 THE CRY NO ONE HEARD

"Hear my cry, O God; attend unto my prayer. From the end of the earth will I cry unto thee, when my heart is overwhelmed: lead me to the rock that is higher than I."

~Psalms 61:1-2

During life people go through and experience many different and sometimes challenging adversities. Whether the lesson to be learned is good or bad, however, to some degree something always comes out of the circumstances of each individual situation. One of my most exhilarating, yet petrifying experiences in my life I would think was my graduation.

It may not have been exciting to some but for kids that were my age at the time, graduating from the 5th grade was such a great accomplishment and we had taken on a huge milestone. Now, we were heading over into the big world of Middle school. Honestly, I guess it's the same with middle school students who are excited and nervous their entire 8th-grade year as they prepare to enter high school.

High school was a little different though because it was without question that friends would be split up and attend different schools. This would make things more difficult for some and not others because of peers, understanding that peer support plays a big factor in a child's excitement and outlook on life.

And then we have the High school students that are extremely excited about their 12th grade year as they are now preparing their exit for "the real world." Now, they are either off to college, trade school, or maybe even off to find a job, or enjoy life.

Growing up in the 80's and 90's graduating from college was considered to be a huge goal and a great accomplishment. In the 2000's it had now become a great accomplishment for those that are fortunate enough to just make it through high school. Because times had changed and there are so many students dropping out and not taking education seriously.

"While the number of low-grad-rate high schools has declined considerably over the past decade, in some states they still predominate" (High School Graduation Facts: Ending the Dropout Crisis, 2018).

Often times I don't think parents realize it takes a lot of time, effort, and dedication to achieve that diploma, not to mention all the peer pressure that comes along with it. Reflecting back, my middle school experience actually was rather rough. I was a very troubled child; even though I tried to hide it. Not only was I struggling with my school work, but I was also silently crying out for help, but no one ever paid me enough attention to sense my pain, nor did they notice the change in my behavior. After my

4th grade year when I was attending Lemoyne Elementary, this girl that I thought I was madly in love with said she was transferring to Grant Middle school. Of course, I transferred too, so I could be there with her. All to find out in the end that her mom had said no "Yikes."

There I was at a school without my boo. From there, I was continuously suspended for fighting, talking back and being disruptive. During the month of February that year I was expelled and shipped to Shea Middle school and I already knew that I would not like it. I had very low self-esteem, self-worth and zero self-confidence.

I've always dealt with being socially awkward, I've always had anxiety, and in more ways than others I have been socially isolated. While in my 8th grade year I experienced something, that I will never forget. One of the hall monitors said something to me that was intended to be an insult however, I took it as a compliment, and it did the complete opposite for me.

I mean how much do words really mean? And after you've endured years of insults you become numb to them. "You will never grow up to be anything in life!" Mr. Brown said to me as he walked by me in the corridor. Deep inside I had already mapped out the different methods I could use to kill him with my bare hands. For the life of me, I couldn't understand how or why an adult would think to talk to a child like that. Regardless of how they acted or what they did in the past. Mr. Brown had no idea that I was on edge that day trying to deal with my father's death, and that I didn't have anyone to talk too.

That Thursday morning was my 8th grade graduation day. The night before I was extremely excited, and I can remember ironing my clothes, cleaning my shoes, and even going as far as brushing my teeth and putting on my clothes that night. So, in the morning all I had to do was just get up and run out of the house. The thought of graduating alone had me excited. The morning finally came, and I woke up at 6:45 am. I don't think I slept much the night before. After a quick shower and brushing my teeth. I washed my face and got dressed. I put on a two-piece three-button black zoot suit. (It was men's suit with high-waisted, wide-legged, tight-cuffed, pegged trousers, and a long coat with wide lapels and wide padded shoulders). I put on a grey shirt and a maroon tie with black shoes to match.

You couldn't tell me I wasn't the cleanest person on the entire planet that day. When I walked out of the house that morning. I heard all types of compliments in my head that didn't actually exist, but they were still good for my confidence. As I walked the three blocks up the hill to Shea Middle school, I practiced my smile, wave, and speech. Just in case, they called me up to speak. As if I weren't one of the worst behaved kids in the whole school.

Sitting in class waiting for the signal and we finally got the call that it was our time to head to the auditorium. All my classmates were excited, and I was too. As we walked down the halls of Shea Middle School, other students saw their grandparents, parents, related children, and staff screaming students' names out as they walked in. My head dropped, and my happiness turned to despair when I noticed that none of my family were there while everyone else was surrounded by family and friends.

Yes, I was bothered in all honesty. Bothered because I was embarrassed and ashamed that everyone else had people bring flowers and gifts to take pictures with. They were loved by their family members and I had no one. I walked out of the building directly after the ceremony was over. Walking past everyone that was too happy to notice my disappointment. Once I made it to the top of the hill I cried all the way down.

I desired to be like the rest of the kids in my class and I wanted to be celebrated too, but that wasn't my experience. When I made it home I walked past everyone with my suit on and no one even thought to ask. I stayed in my room for majority of the day refusing to greet or interact with anyone because I was that angry, hurt, and upset.

I could tell by the way I ended my eighth-grade year that my first day of ninth grade would be challenging. There would be greater expectations than there were in the eighth grade, and the teachers would be much stricter. I was also afraid that my classmates had changed over the summer. Some had gotten taller, prettier, or even smarter. Leaving me to be the only senseless ugly duckling that refused to evolve.

But overall, I missed everyone over the summer, and that helped me forget all about my worries of returning to school after the summer break. On the evening before school, I prepared for my big day. My backpack was filled with everything I needed to be a success. I had new notebooks, binders, pens, pencils, and of course a few snacks because I was quite the hefty guy. As time continued to tick, I could feel the anxiety growing inside of me. Growing impatient I asked myself while looking at the clock on the wall, when is school going to start? Will my nerves ever calm down? Either way, I just wished that the first day of school would hurry up and come so that I could get it over with.

It was finally time to go to school and I remember that day like it was today. I awakened just as I had done on any other school day, but I was just a little more excited. This was my very first day at Fowler High School. I took the city bus to school that morning with my new school clothes on, and I was hyped up about seeing all my friends. Walking into high school was so different that I was a little shocked.

Things were completely different now. I was older, I had matured, and I kept telling myself that this year was going to be a better year. I had no clue that I would actually have to live up to my words. This year I would have to put work in and change my behavior if I wanted success. My first half of the day everything was normal. But then during 1st lunch, everything had gotten better because I was able to see my friends.

Texting on our phones without getting in trouble for having them was one of our main goals as students, and I can't lie school was fun. But my high school year took a wrong turn when my behavior started getting out of control. Honestly, I didn't even know what to do in order to change it. A few months into my 9th grade school year I was kicked out and sent to a behavior alternative program until the end of year.

If that wasn't bad enough I was failing nearly all my classes. Mr. Brown's words started to echo in my mind as I realized that I was living up to the words he spoke to me back in middle school. As anger set in, I decided that I needed to make a change, and I became grateful for the mandated counseling sessions. Four days a week was ordered by the court and I didn't oppose it because I needed someone to vent to.

I finished out my freshman year in behavioral school and now it was time for me to start the 10th grade at Corcoran Highschool. I barely knew anyone there and I hardly ever talked to anyone. Other than the select few friends I made, I stuck to myself because I was determined not to get into any more trouble.

By the grace of God, I accomplished just that. I managed to never get suspended or get into any more trouble. My grades weren't the best. They were fairly good. And although I struggled with the schoolwork. I kept asking for help, but no one seemed to notice or have time for my inadequacy.

For years my classmates and I got excited about the festivities that comes with being a senior such as senior dinner, senior skip day and of course the biggest of them all Prom and graduation, we would always say I can't wait for senior year. Now that our senior year was underway, we began to feel as if time was flying by too fast as we needed to complete schoolwork, find a prom date and what we were going to wear to prom of course. It was extremely hard for me to find a prom date as I was 6'3 and a whopping 295lbs, I felt that no one would ever be attracted to me, one of my friends who I had the biggest crush mentioned how she didn't enjoy her prom because of the customs of her church and we agreed that she would go with me. On the day of prom, I had honestly one of the prettiest prom dates in the room but prom to me was whack as she spent a great portion of her time with her boyfriend (the one I didn't know she had) on the phone. My feelings were already hurt because a friend of mines had already mentioned that she was telling people that I begged her to come to prom with me, needless to say, I was over prom; I didn't go to the after-party no food or anything I dropped her off to the hotel and went out with my friends.

Soon after what every senior has been waiting for, for 13 years well in my case 14 years as I had failed the first grade due to my attendance was graduation. My classmates and I were so excited to receive our caps and gowns and to attend graduation rehearsal, it was just surreal. Well, I felt my life come crumbling down when I got the news that I did not pass Global 10 state test and would not be graduating with the rest of my class, I was reassured that it wasn't a big deal and if I attended summer school I would be able to graduate in August, I felt better about it and didn't stress it. I attended summer school every steaming hot day with no air conditioning or fans and still failed the test again. I had to figure out what to do quickly as I was embarrassed and ashamed that I was not going to be graduating, speaking with my counselor she informed me I would be able to take the test during state testing the next scholastic school year; this wasn't a big deal as I had no intentions on going to college; I never had anyone mention college to me or it's importance ever that I can recall other than my 10th grade English teacher. Well to skip through I had taken this global exam which was a pain in my hindsight and still had not passed this stupid exam, by this time I had begun researching colleges as I wanted to be something different than my surroundings, my friends and cousins weren't doing anything and I knew that I was different than them, I always said I'm cut from a precious cloth they no longer sell. I was a bit discouraged at this point if I was, to be honest, I began to google different things and trying to find out what I could do, I signed up to take my GED and had no money to afford the exam, I lied to a close friend and borrowed money and I bombed the GED exam 2 times; I felt worthless, dumb, stupid, retarded and any other words one could use to describe someone that's incompetent and stupid; but yet I still hadn't told anyone in my family that I didn't graduate; oh wait did I forget to mention I had a big graduation cookout thrown by mom but no one even took the time out to realize they had never attended my high school graduation or seen any pictures of it. I soon found out a local community college offered a program where you could earn your GED while attending the college, this gave me hope, well I drove my 1990 green intrepid that I could only put $5 of gas in it at a time as I had a gas line break to the college to take the entrance placement exam and I failed. I began to research other colleges and found out that Mohawk Valley Community College offered the same program and I was determined to get in; I caught the greyhound there and got accepted into the program which was one of the happiest days of my life.

Can you imagine how it feels to have no support as a young man from your family? Can you imagine how it feels to be a part of a family that never showed up to any events, showed any concern, wouldn't know what school you attended, where you live at or who your closest friends are.

Often times we as humans misbehaving is not essentially analyzed to figure out precisely why the person is doing it. We must first take time to understand the derivation cause of those exasperating, frustrating, maddening behaviors. Too many times we fail to admit but we all (humans) have a need for belonging and worth. Honestly, it's just the way in which the human body is set up. When we feel a sense of belonging along with positive attention from others it forms a sense of emotional connection. When a person doesn't feel a strong bond of belonging, they will oftentimes begin to act out in ways that they believe they will get a form of emotional connection and positive attention they crave.

CHAPTER 5: IS IT MY FAULT?

*"How long, O Lord? Will you forget me forever?
How long will you hide your face from me? How
long must I take counsel in my soul and have sorrow
in my heart all the day?*

~Psalm 13 ESV

While Growing up I always thought and knew that I was special even at the early age of six years old. I thought that I had come from a great American family, because most of my family members were doing awesome things in their own perspectives. I have no doubt that my parents loved me. Not to mention I was extremely spoiled being the only child. Truth be told, both sides of my family have long histories with substance abuse disorder. Today, I'm a thirty-two-year-old man, unfortunately still dealing with 28 years of built-up frustration. I was still stuck in the maximum-security prison of my mind I am deeply distressed about what has been done to me by people that I trusted, and my parents trusted, yet they deceived us.

Throughout our existent whether we know it or not we are influenced and taught by many different people. What we learn can easily have an effect on the manner in which we view and handle difficulties and proceedings within communal boundaries. It is my belief that the most significant and effective influences that children have in their lives come from their families. Family dynamics can have equally

71

positive and negative influences on their lives. If you were desiring to comprehend my family, I would tell you to imagine a superlative 50's sitcom family with a 90's attitude.

To just be honest I don't think there are many people that have ever met a family quite like mine. My family is somewhat different and very dysfunctional. Each family member plays a central and critical role in the family system. Whether their role is a vital role or a nonexistent role nevertheless they do in fact exist. After years of hearing my family members speak so negatively about my mother, I started to resent them at an early age.

My parents' actions personally influenced how I behaved as a child. They also affected how I felt and acted towards others and the outside world. I think that if a child is brought up with hatred, anger and or violence, they will view the world in a highly negative way. Often resulting in them being treacherous and bias towards others. However, if a child is raised with love, compassion, and acts of kindness their outlook will be different. Even if there is a mixture of negative and positive things going on in the household that the child is exposed to. Eventually the child will decide for themselves which path they will choose. Some may say that my words sound silly, but I would have to disagree because it is my life and my exact experience. And for me, I chose to do the exact opposite of what I witnessed growing up.

Over time I've heard numerous clichés that more than often proved to be true. Like "everything happens for a reason," that was my favorite one. Now, that I am fully grown for some reason I no longer believe in that saying. I think things happen for one or two reasons, however, habitually we tend to blame one thing, while blind eyeing the other. My family was always open to voice about their past drug use, but you would never hear anyone talk about abuse that came with the addiction. Rather it was emotional, physical, and or sexual. To be honest the majority of them had their share of the physically abusive aspect at one point. My upbringing was a classic case of misdirection (according to Webster dictionary misdirection means the action or process of directing someone to the wrong place or in the wrong direction.)

The world we live in is full of doubt, insecurity, and fear. And as bad as I desired, hoped, prayed, and wished that my family would always be there for me, that just wasn't my reality. Them holding their arms open and welcoming me with love was just a wish I had that never came true. Although, I could never say that none of my family was ever there for me. I'll be clear and say that it was very few. Throughout my life there were times when I didn't want to go to school because I had butterflies in my stomach, and I found it problematic to walk. I was just always so panicky. School was quite difficult for me in all areas ranging from academics to social behavior. I was a big dreamer and if I was being told off, I would just switch my brain off and drift to another place. Whenever I was being teased or bullied, I would switch off as well and I spent most of my school days feeling detached and isolated from those around me.

Developing mentally and physically in an environment that doesn't provide value and encouragement only constant insults, left me feeling belittled and bashed every day and it had a tremendous negative impact on my childhood life. I was always called gay, pus*y, faggot, and any other offensive names by family members, school mates, and even my own father at one point. No one realized that my femininity had not one thing to do with my sexuality. Why was it my fault I rarely had a male role model in my life to teach me the ropes of manhood? One that loved me enough to take me under their wing, love me, train me, and teach me the things I didn't know. Is it my fault that my father was in prison and absent from my life as I was thrown to the wolves? Is it my fault that my grandfather didn't love me enough to want to be around me? And is it my fault that my Uncles weren't concerned or active? I never had any other role models in my life outside of my Bishop and my godfather the late Elder Melvin Ryans. The two of them always took me to men's retreats, dinner or just to hang out. They knew I never had money, so they would pay for it, and as much as I tried it was impossible to learn everything from them.

People don't realize the negative impact they have on others when they downgrade them with words. I was more feminine than the average boy, it wasn't something I wanted, it was just how I was. I cried many days and nights because I had gotten sick of

BROKEN

hearing people call me out of my name. I had grown tired of being classified and placed in a certain category because I didn't walk straight. I had a high pitch tone in my voice and many of my close friends were all females. As I grew older I just wanted to be "normal." Or what was considered to be normal but instead I tried my best to stay away from all men. My trust level when it came to men was minimal because most of my experiences with them were negative. Something in me hated men with every fiber of my soul. I'm not sure who's to blame but I am grown now, and I still struggle with building healthy relationships with men for this reason. I'm not using it as a crutch I'm just being honest.

I am going to share one of those experiences with you, so you'll have a better idea of where I am

78

coming from. Let's call him Bill. He was established in his career, undistinguished in appearance and demeanor, and there was nothing about him that made him stand out in a crowd. Bill was someone I trusted, and I allowed him in my inner space while coming to our brown and white two-family home sitting at the dead-end of Elk Street in Syracuse, NY. I remembered this house because this is where he would handle odds and ends for my father. Bill sat me down on the edge of the bed, unzipped his pants, and began to masturbate in front of me. Then he grabbed my hand and made me touch him. And this is how I first learned about sex. After that, I started hating everyone although I never verbalized it, I was angry on the inside and no one ever recognized that there was something wrong or different about me. Even though everything about me had changed. The way I smiled, laughed, and even held conversations. But it didn't end there.

The first-day bill raped me I was 10 years old, it started with him complimenting me on how I was growing up to be an attractive young man. Then when my parents were out and about he ripped off my pants, then my underwear, and started ramming his penis in me right in the living room. I can still feel his crusty hands on me forcibly holding me down. I can still smell the cheap scent of Old Spice and I can still feel the agony, pain, and disgust in my body. If that wasn't enough he terrorized me and forced me into silence. He never used a weapon or threat, yet I was trapped in a mental prison. Bill promised me and convinced me that if I ever said anything, people would call me gay and my family wouldn't love me anymore. In fear of rejection, I kept my mouth shut and tried my hardest to remain silent for years. I hid behind my eyes and stopped looking directly into the eyes of anyone for fear that they would view me as having some kind of sickness or perversion inside of me. I didn't want to be hated or rejected. For years I had the feeling of wallowing in a bottommost black pit, and no matter how hard I tried to free myself I just couldn't see the top.

On a Saturday night in 2005 while I was working at the Burger King in midway, I was in the back doing prep and I heard a voice that sounded familiar to me. I instantly froze. I just stopped what I was doing while my supervisor kept calling my name. She said that I looked as if I had died and come back to life while standing there. When I was finally able to formulate my words, I looked at her and told her that I had to go. I put my head down and ran out the kitchen pass the front counter. The run to my 1992 Grey Buick seemed so far away. I got in my car while hyperventilating and panicking. My first reaction was to call my childhood best friend Joey. The moment he answered I just started screaming crying. I didn't know how to feel or react to hearing Bill's voice. Because the truth was that he was well and alive and not dead or in jail for what he did to me.

Eventually, I had to admit the fact that I would never be severed from the abuse and pain caused by his actions. So why is it my fault that it resulted in defining me? It was because of him that my behavior in school was disruptive and I was mandated by the court to attend counseling. Throughout my entire time in high school I had to take anger management and they all said it was my fault and nothing seemed to help. After attending counseling 4 days a week for 2 years straight, I never made any progress. And I was still locked up inside of my trauma, unable to free myself. Of course, I know that the abuse will never disappear on its own and I still have some bad days, panic attacks, flashbacks, and anxiety. Especially when I'm around unfamiliar people. But now, I have far more good days than bad, and thank God, the abuse no longer rules my life regardless of who thought is it my fault.

The good news is that when I was in my mid 20's, I met a girl who changed my life. She opened my eyes to a fragment of a new world and a portion of life that I had no clue even existed. By now I had experienced plenty of girlfriends. I slept with multiple people recklessly trying to prove a point to my own heart, mind, body, and soul. But this girl was different, and slowly but surely, she won my entire heart over. This was the first time that I ever fallen in love, and it was the deepest love I had ever felt. I honestly didn't know that a person could feel such incredible happiness on one hand and actually be miserable on the other.

I've now come to the realization that finding what we call the right person, in which we classify as the person we want to spend the rest of our lives with, is by far one of the greatest achievements in life. Yet, the ill-fated truth is that the right person doesn't always derive at the right time. And that makes all the difference in the world. My life instantly changed for the better. I had seen it in the movies before where a couple meets and the suddenly falls in love, then they live happily ever after. But I didn't honestly think it was real and I always thought how delightful it would be if finding true love was just that simple.

In reality, we are emotionally intricate and because we're so emotionally complicated, we manage to make situations complicated. We must be cognizant even when we do find the right person, if we ourselves are not the right person in which we need to be the relationship will not be successful no matter how cute you two look together, how many children you have, how much of a power couple you are it won't work. Typically, one would collapse emotionally and unfortunately, take it out on the person you love. There is no difference for the person in which you love, the same concept applies, if he or she isn't at the point in their life where they can be devoted, faithful, committed, and loving to their partner the relationship will fail; as surely as snow is white. There are so many ways a relationship can fail, it's amazing that we aren't all alone.

I tried my hardest to do everything in my power I knew, things I seen my Bishop and Godfather do with their wives because that was the only real relationship I had ever seen, additionally things that I googled to ensure I was the ideal boyfriend. I never once tried to negate the fact that I was hurting inside because of what had happened to me, but I was trying hard to supersede that feeling as I had fell in love with this girl with my entire whole heart. Let's talk about her for a minute, (let's call her Teesha), she was not the nicest person not at all, did she have the Coca-Cola body shape not at all, was she hood absolutely (lol) but one thing she did do was love the hell out of me with all of her being, she covered me, prayed for and with me, told me when she thought I was watching tv too much and I needed to pull away and focus on the mission at hand, she cooked a homemade meal for me at least 4 days a week and the other days we ate out. I wasn't looking for the perfect person at all, as I knew that didn't really exist, she wasn't perfect but everything within me kept telling me she was perfect for me.

When I was out of work for an injury and didn't have funds to pay for us to go out to eat with friends like we were used to, she would give me her debit card in the car to protect my pride so I was still able to pay for the meal. Wherever I went to speak she was there front and center, the loudest person in the room and my biggest supporter. I can recall the time I was hospitalized while attending college in buffalo NY, I called her that night to complain really quick because I was scared but most certainly was not going to tell her that.

I woke up the next morning she was there along with my other friends. It didn't end right there, I ended up taking leave from college and going back home to my mothers, she was at my mother's house with me every day feeding me, aiding me hand and foot, when the Drs prescribed me medicine that was too strong and I couldn't stay awake for more than 15 minutes at a time she was there even while I slept for days. Reading all of that you would think wow why did this guy end up not marrying her, what is wrong, wait is he "gay" but in reality, there were somethings that I never had to address with anyone because I had never loved anyone as much as her. One Thursday evening we broke up, after years of not speaking when we did finally talk we both had different reasons why we no longer wanted to be in the relationship together; for months after we separated I kept thinking is it my fault we're not together or is it her fault, can I blame her and not me, I don't want to take the blame for it at all. It wasn't until roughly year two after we broke up that I was able to accept that it was merely on both of us split in the middle, she had her reason which I didn't agree with fully of why she was done and my reasoning she didn't really accept either.

Letting a person go you love is most difficult. Have you ever taken a moment and thought about it; the longer you are apart from each other the more you come to realize how tough it is, the more you understand how much you actually love that person. I wouldn't dare allow my pride to get in the way and act as if I didn't still know that a part of me does, and always will, love her. Thinking about a person every day of your life, the one you picked out the ring for and was just waiting for a specific event to pop the question although you were terrified of marriage. Thinking about that person that you had made plans to enjoy life with knowing that you know you will never be with is a hell of its own. But you learn to manage.

Can I speak to you as the reader for a moment? I earnestly pray that you have the strength not only to keep going but not to give up on yourself. At one point or another we all have had to give up on a job, a friend or even a relationship with a person you just knew this was it, but you can find love again/make it.

You must believe in you, no one will believe in you more than you do; and the fact that you can overcome it because it is possible. I must believe that it will happen for me just as you have to believe it will happen for you.

CHAPTER 6: I WANT TO
FORGIVE, BUT HOW?

As human beings some of us tend to be more naturally inclined to anger than others, and unfortunately, we tend to place blame on those whom we feel have done us wrong. Most people would say that it takes a lot of effort to let go and even more effort to forgive. Too often we don't realize that we are suppressing the pain that we actually feel deep down inside. But then again, at this point who's really to blame? Is it the perpetrator or the victim that holds on to the pain and never releases it?

Sadly, more often than not, as people we continuously allow the same person that hurt us to hurt us over and over again. We allow them to constantly belittle us, and do us wrong. Honestly, it's quite strange the way that the dopamine in our brains play a role in how and why we allow people to hurt us. Dopamine is a known chemical messenger inside of the brain, technically known as a neurotransmitter. Responsible for sending signals directly from the central nervous system. For example, have you ever wondered why we often act surprised at countless occurrences throughout life in which we tend to act masochistically towards ourselves?

Letting go of pain seems to be perplexed but in reality, it's simple. One must forgive and then try their best to forget. As hard as it may seem, you must forgive those that have wronged you, and you must forgive yourself. Someone years ago, said to me "Forgiveness is not for them however, it is for you." And I'm writing my story because I wanted to share some of the pain, frustration, and hurt I've had to endure over the years. Even though I wouldn't change any of it now that I am grown because it definitely shaped me into who I am today.

Daddy's Boy

I will never forget May 1, 2002. I was 14 years old to be exact and that night I went to sleep and dreamed that my Gramz, the most consistent, important person in my life passed away. I woke up in a frenzy, crying, and sweating but I held everything in and told no one about my nightmare. Without saying a word to my mother, I got ready for school and left to start my day. The next day which was Thursday May 2, my mom came to pick me up from school which was very rare, so I should have known that something was wrong. None of my family ever came to my school for anything at all. Even when I had gotten suspended it was done over the telephone and then I walked home. My mother was standing in the office wearing a pair of boxer shorts, an orange tank top, and her hair was wrapped up in a used pair of panties. We got in the car and she took me to Burger King before breaking the news to me.

"Your father passed away, Honey."

It didn't bother me right away for some reason and I'm not sure why, possibly because at that moment it just hadn't registered.

Church was all I ever knew so I went to church that night for bible study and my Bishop mentioned to the church about the passing of my father. But it wasn't until he started teaching about folks dying daily that I ran out of the sanctuary and completely lost it. I just felt like my life was over because I had never dealt with death so close to me. The death of my father hit home and struck every nerve in my body. Not to mention that my father was a Buddhist my entire childhood, and he worshiped the Buddhist figurine, in addition to performing animal sacrifices that he never let me join. But regardless of any of that, I wanted to be just like my dad, Eventually, before my dad passing, he had started coming to church with me and had even made plans to get baptized in the name of Jesus Christ and according to Acts 2:38.

We were planning to buy matching suits for my birthday which was right around the corner and now, suddenly, he was gone. And to think that for years following his death, I hated him because as a kid he promised me that he would never leave me again once he got out of prison. He had missed out on so much of my life already and then "bam" he was gone again, and this time it would be forever. For ten years straight, I cried myself to sleep several nights just being angry, hateful, bitter & spiteful. For ten long years I was angry at God and my father. But then I started visiting my father's gravesite to let things out. And after crying time and time again I was able to release the anger I had built over the years, and boy did I feel a ton better. I still cry some days. Especially around birthdays and for me things have never been the same since 2002. It changed me forever.

I remained in shock throughout the duration of my dad's funeral service. All I can remember hearing were cries of sorrow. I had already made up in my mind that my father was gone and that I would have to be strong for my mother and little sister. I recall looking around the church and realizing that the church was packed. Filled by people we hadn't seen in ages and people I knew that never meant my father any good. I kept shutting my eyes tightly and slowly reopening them hoping that someone would tell me that it was a bad dream or a terrible joke. But they didn't, and this was my reality.

I know that I undoubtedly seemed fine on the outside, but internally I was dying and torn apart at every angle. During the eulogy, I listened closely to the message because I needed to keep my mind off the fact that my dad was lying dead in a casket directly in front of me. Moments later once the Preacher was done, the casket closed, and I cried so hard that I wanted to vomit. I had to face the reality that my Dad was really gone forever. Before I knew it, I slipped into a deep depression. Once everyone got to the burial site, I wanted to close my eyes, but I knew that one day I would regret not seeing the whole ceremony. So, I opened my eyes and saw the rose petals dropping on top of the casket as my bishop said,

"From ashes to ashes, and dust to dust." I knew then that it was all over.

Everything around me started to move rapidly, and I was no longer daddy's little boy. I was now being forced to grasp things in a different way. Before long, I realized that I had to turn my negative into something positive, if not I wouldn't make it in life. And, all that my father ever wanted for me in life is exactly what I endeavor for now. The death of my father has motivated me and inspired me to strive for greatness. Ironically, his death aided me in becoming the person I am today. I'm glad to say that I am independent, I enjoy the better things in life, and I'm proud to be his only son.

Why Granddad Why

There's a special kind of bond that resides between a grandfather and his grandson. And honestly, there's nothing quite like it. Most of my childhood is filled with memories that don't include my grandfather at all. But from what people told me he was a great man. Although I don't doubt he was a great man to them but unfortunately, I just cannot personally say the same. Some of the things I do know is that he was a church deacon, he worked as a driver for Centro public transportation buses in the city of Syracuse, N.Y., and ever since I have known of his existence, even living in the same city as my mother and I neither of us ever had ever spent any time with him. He was a tall handsome older man, that stood about 6'2 and weighs about 185lbs with dark skin. He was a guy that was always well dressed and unfortunately always full of lies.

I recall times when my mother and I would take the Centro bus because we didn't have a car and that was our only means of transportation. I knew that my grandfather would be driving a bus near where I was, and I would literally chase his bus down until I couldn't run anymore or he was gone completely out of my sight. Some days I would catch his bus just to see him and I remember always being extremely excited to finally catch up with him. Just for him to lie telling me how much he loved me and how he still had my birthday gift from the prior year. It never failed whenever I saw him he would tell the same lie. Now I'm 32 years of age and still have yet to receive one single gift from him.

One summer his family had a family reunion over on Cortland Ave in Syracuse NY and for some reason my mom decided that she wanted to go. I didn't want to go at all, but my mom and sister wanted to go. When we arrived at the white and blue house sitting across from one of the oldest Apostolic churches in the Syracuse area, we walked through the gate to the backyard where everyone was drinking beer, eating food, and playing cards. It seemed like the world froze when we walked in. A few family members who my mother still had a good standing relationship with came over and welcomed us while introducing us to other people that were there. I noticed that they introduced my mother as just Stacy and not as Stacy Louis's daughter, which made me a little uncomfortable to be there. To fill in the gap, my mother was one of two children that my grandfather Louis had outside of his marriage. As a result, they hated us, even though his adulterous actions weren't our fault. It had absolutely nothing to do with us. No longer than 45 minutes later of us being at the function we were told that we needed to leave right away. My mom cried for days because of this, and she very seldom discussed her feelings about how her dad's wife and daughters all treated her. All she ever wanted was to be accepted by her father just as any child would. Personally, I had thoughts of making a scene and shutting down the entire function by knocking over the four grills that were cooking the ribs, chicken, steak, sausages, and seafood boil. I wanted to take my slow time flipping over each table and punching every person there whether they were nice or not. My intentions were to destroy the entire event for everyone because they were mistreating my mother.

Years later Louis was in the hospital and not doing so well. One of my cousins on his side contacted my mother with the news and just like every other time she broke her neck to get to his rescue. And of course, his very angry, spiteful, hateful wife was there which made it impossible for my mom to actually go in to visit him. My mother decided to call him on the phone and she was finally able to speak with him. I was happy for her and I had never wished any bad on him or even really had any ill feelings toward him other than being confused about why he treated us the way he did. My mother sat on the phone with him like a little school girl smiling from ear to ear excited about talking to her father. She let him know that she wanted to come and check on him, and he told her that she can call up to the hospital anytime. He instructed her to say that she's one of the nurses and to give a false name. The way my mother cried after that conversation with him was like nothing I'd ever seen before. For the first time, I wished he died a painful, excruciating death for hurting my mothers' feelings once again. While most have heard that having a strong male influence is vital in a little boy's life, I would like to say that a male influence in the life of a child regardless of their sex is crucial.

On the other hand, a constructive father-daughter relationship tends to have an enormous impression on a young girl's life and will even regulate whether or not she develops into a strong, confident woman. A father's influence in his daughter's life often time shapes her self-esteem, self-image, confidence, and opinions of men.

Another Good-Bye

What children need utmost are the rudiments that their grandmother provides in copiousness. Grandmothers give unrestricted comfort, humor, kindness, love, patience, and lessons in life. Well at least mine did. Words cannot express how much my Gramz means to me. She not only shows the talents of a hero, but she is my hero. Most importantly she possessed the qualities of an amazing grandmother.

Gramz has been revered all her life, being the eldest of four children, it was a struggle to get even the smallest amount of attention. Even though she was only one of the three that were left, she still took the time to remember and laugh about her childhood.

My Gramz truly deserved a much better life than the one that was handed to her. Yet she barely complained. She kept nurturing the positive out of me as time went by. I have lived with my Gramz all my life until I grew up and moved out to live in a different city. The stuff that I saw my Gramz endure was beyond crazy. There were times when we went months without having running water in our house and we had to run a hose from her neighbor, who was a very close friend of the family. We would get rides to and from the church by a variety of people. And my Bishop at one point had set it up for one of the deacons to drop us off because he lived on the next street over.

One time we rode with the Deacon on a cold winter night and he made us get out at the corner and walk the rest of the way to our house. Not to mention my entire life my Gramz only wore skirts because it was our religion. Our family members very rarely came by to visit her. Not even later on in life when she was sick and ended up in the hospital. They barely called on birthdays and Holidays. Someone in our family that was very close to my Gramz even stole her brand-new truck she paid cash for, and because of who they were she never pressed charges against them. She did things like put her house up to get someone out of jail and ended up losing her home behind it. At a young age, Gramz taught me to be brave, to follow my heart, and to never give up no matter what difficulty may be discouraging you. At the age of fifty-six Gramz decided she was going to attend college although she had only made it to the fifth grade. I loved her ambition. If nothing else, Gramz was determined. She caught the Centro bus back and forth to her college campus with heavy books in her backpack, but she didn't let that stop her. She had family members that constantly stole from her and she still showed them love every chance she could get. My Gramz would beg me not to say anything to people who offended her, she always wanted to keep the peace. Even up until the recent days, but I preferred to hurt them for her.

I'll never forget driving down Highway 280 in Birmingham, Alabama heading to work. It was Monday morning June 12, 2017, and my phone rung at 8:37, it was my mother. I answered the phone to her crying hysterically and I could barely understand anything she was saying. I kept asking what was wrong and finally she blurted it out,

"Mommy's gone, she's dead!"

At a loss for words, I hung up the phone on her and closed my eyes. I was driving and crying extremely hard. I wanted to drive my car over a bridge and die with her. I don't think anyone will ever understand the pain I felt that day My Gramz was my best friend. We did everything together, and she was a fighter and a survivor. Gramz was goofy, and at times annoying, but she was the best cook I have ever known. She was an excessive talker and all around the most beautiful person I ever knew. She radiated with poise and elegance. My Gramz made me feel loved beyond measure, and I consider her not only the most influential person of my childhood, but of my entire life thus far. That day at work was extremely hard for me because I couldn't stop crying. Every couple of minutes, the tears began to fall, and I didn't want to be bothered. But I knew I couldn't go home alone because I was scared. I had never thought about taking my own life until this day. It was literally one of the hardest things I have ever had to endure. We were so close that if my Gramz was a kangaroo, I would be the little one inside her pouch.

The Death of my Gramz transformed my identity, and my sense of independence was completely shattered when my Gramz departed from my life, this experience devastated my perspective on life and what it meant to live. Losing a loved one felt like having a wisdom tooth pulled without any Novocain. I still think of my Gramz every single day and I often think of all that she endured and went through. She worked extremely hard to give my family and myself the life that we enjoy today. I eventually moved back to Syracuse NY to ensure that I was close to where my Gramz was buried as I knew that no one in my family would take care of her the way that I would. To this very day, I make sure that I visit her a few times a week making sure her gravesite is neat and well kept. The grief still comes at random times, and even lingers on for days. The truth is that she never leaves my mind, and I love my grandma more than anyone I have ever loved in my entire life.

Most importantly, I have my grandmother's recollection deeply embedded in my heart, mind, & soul. Even though it may not be in the physical realm she will forever be in my mind, and spirit pushing me to be the handpicked, cream of the crop that I am capable of being.

A hero is someone who has given their life to something bigger than oneself. Most heroes are athletes, celebrities, or movie stars. They are known for being famous or making a lot of money. To me, none of that matters, because I've already had the best hero in the world my entire life. My Gramz.

CHAPTER 7:
WHO AM I?

"The truth is, we all face hardships of some kind, and you never know the struggles a person is going through. Behind every smile, there's a story of a personal struggle"

~ Adrienne C. Moore

A precarious task we face in life is figuring out who we really are. It may be one of life's simplest questions for a lot of people. Meanwhile, on the other hand, it can be one of the most difficult questions to answer for some. For those of us that are confused when we're asked directly to describe ourselves, our minds tend to draw a blank. For some reason, we can't find the proper terms to fully sum ourselves up. We find ourselves in need of prompts and suggestions from others that help us discover who we are or organize a clear picture of ourselves.

Often, we just avoid answering the question at all. Then there are times when we tend to laugh about it, or we may simply ask others to tell us in their words. Additionally, we may even go to the extent of being silent and waiting for others to answer for us. More often than not we constantly ask ourselves every day that we look in the mirror. "Who am I?" And ironically no one can answer the question. Not even us. Even while you're reading my words I am quite sure that the majority of you have already given up on finding an answer. Whether you are six years old or one hundred years old you're still in search of your identity or your purpose.

Some may ask why we never found ourselves. But for me, I describe "Who I am" at the end of the book. I believe there's so much more in which we can learn about ourselves and others just from sharing and reading about the stories of the past. When we share our life's experiences in ways that help others we can keep people from making the same mistakes and inspire others to see their way through. This is extremely true when it comes to my life. When explaining my life to someone I would sum it up by saying my life has been an extremely interesting roller coaster of emotions, some good, some great, and a ton of bad moments. But I saw my way through.

As I have grown and matured over the years there have been various aspects of my life that have inclined me to do certain things, and make certain decisions. As a result of some of my choices, I am who I am today. And with that, I can confidently say that of course, everything in life isn't perfect, and every aspect of my life is not yet settled: however, I am on the path to living my best life ever in its early stages.

Many people may wonder who I am on the inside, outside of the things I've written about I have been transparent throughout this entire book. I am the eldest child of Sylvio and Stacy Rodriguez, and since my father's passing my mother has remarried and is now married to Ralph young. I am the eldest of four children. I have one sister, Glady, and two brothers named Jeremiah & Daniel. I am the proud father of a four-year-old son name Davion, who at an early age has already traveled the world more than most of my counterparts at my current age, in addition I am the foster father for two other young men, one of the boys is one years old and the other is eight years old. We have lived/traveled in Germany, Oklahoma, Puerto Rico, Dominican Republic, and quite a few other places in this short span of life thus far.

Looking back, I was a kid that grew up spending the majority of my life feeling like I was never enough. Mainly because for most of my life I was overweight. I also suffered from low self-esteem, minimal self-worth, and no self-confidence. I can hardly recall anyone ever affirming anything positive to me throughout my life. And, I always felt as though I wasn't smart enough, my teeth were all jacked up, my voice was too high, and to top it off I was more feminine than the females around me. Throughout elementary school all the way up through college I always felt that everyone else was better than me, smarter than me, and more attractive than me. Being that I was the one so often times overlooked, underestimated, underappreciated, taken for granted, taken advantage of, abused, and misused by others, I never understood that my self-worth was non-negotiable. I am the kid that grew up in the hood without any educational mentors and I was the one that everyone talked down too. But God still saw fit to keep his hand on me throughout my life and all the things that I have been through. Today, I'm a survivor, and an educator previously taught secondary education and changing lives daily.

Over time, multiple events will take place that will eventually force one to grow and become more mature. In my case, I have undergone five major situations that caused my transformation and for personal reasons, I will only talk about one that changed my entire life drastically. This event deals with the passing away of someone who was very important to me and taught me treasured valuable life lessons.

I am who I am today because of my Gramz Bobbie Mae Kaigler. My Gramz is the one person that was there for me every step of the way up until the day she died. She did everything in her power to ensure that I was uplifted and supported. There was no question that I was her favorite grandchild. In all actuality, I have always been more like my Gramz son than her grandson, and she was the best friend I had ever had. She knew all of my secrets and she still loved me undeniably, and unconditionally. We did everything together from praying, reading the bible, fasting, cooking, fishing, going to church, and going trash-picking on college campuses (don't judge us because we often found some great stuff). We even used to catch the bus to Walmart for Black Friday shopping every Thanksgiving. Can you imagine catching the bus to go shopping at Walmart and having to stand in lines for hours in the freezing cold just so Gramz could get all her grandchildren Christmas gifts?

I remember one occasion when our neighbor (Ron) who was one of my Gramz closest friends was in the hospital on his death bed and left his car with my Gramz. It was for her to use while he was in the hospital sick. My great aunt Louise and Gramz planned to go fishing and asked if I wanted to come. I said no, knowing that I had an agenda of my own already planned for the day. I planned to drive Ron's car around in our neighborhood, but I had a little experience driving. I remember waiting until they left before I jumped in the car and began driving down the street. In the beginning, I was doing fine, and everyone was jealous because I was driving. I circled the block about four times and as I was heading south down the street a neighbor yelled my name and startled me. Not knowing how to drive I didn't stop the car before turning around to see what she was calling me for and I ran smack into the fire hydrant, I desperately tried to hide it from my Gramz day after day when she would allow me to move the car from one side of the street to the other because of alternate parking. Eventually, she found out, and even though I disappointed her with my dishonesty she never stopped showing me, love. She disciplined me but loved me at the same time, and I could tell.

My Gramz was and will always be my best friend. My Gramz passed away in 2017 and it was the worst thing that had ever happened to me in my entire existence. I thought losing my dad was hard on me but losing my Gramz brought my entire world to an end. Superheroes in movies, novels, and comic books never die, and she was my superhero. I wanted her to live forever. Although we discussed her passing a thousand times I still wasn't ready, and never will be. After my Gramz left this world I was lost, and I had no clue how I would continue my life without her. Yes, she drove me nuts at times, but I didn't care because she was my Gramz. The one that covered me, prayed for me, fed me, coached me, pushed me, and was always my ultimate supporter. After her transition, I knew based on the decisions I had begun making that I was severely depressed and in need of some serious help. There was no question that I needed to see a psychiatrist. After being diagnosed with anxiety because of the things that were going on in my head. I had mapped out several different ways to commit suicide. I just wanted to end it all and go to a place where I wouldn't have to endure any more pain ever.

So today when someone asks who I am, my response is that I am Ta'Quell W. Morris-Rodriguez, a young kid from the hood who's been hurt, homeless, talked about, abused, misused, mishandled, molested/raped, left for dead and still managed to level up. I am now one of the lead Administrators of color in a city high school. Education is not only who I am but it's literally what I do, I work earnestly to ensure that I am impacting someone along the way. I am somebody.

ABOUT THE AUTHOR

Ta'Quell Morris-Rodriguez, CCDP, M.Ed. is a writer, and author of the new novel *"Broken,"* an entrepreneur, and orator. *Ta'Quell has a master's in education leadership & Business Management from*

BROKEN

Southern New Hampshire University, additionally Ta'Quell obtained a Bachelors Degree in child Welfare Administration & Human Resource Administration. Ta'Quell is a native of Syracuse, NY. Ta'Quell delivers messages of hope, positivity and empowerment that are sustaining and motivating to individuals across the world. His two mottos are "If God said it whether I believe it or not, that settles it" and "It's better to train up whole children than to fix broken adults" encourages us to reach back and help the next generation who will carry us forward.

Ta'Quell can usually be found mentoring, motivating, and encouraging others to become their best selves. Ta'Quell's story is living proof that success is not necessarily about resources. It is merely about being quick-witted and creative. It is about the choice to charge ahead despite the challenges and detractors. Ta'Quell is an acclaimed keynote speaker, motivational speaker, and certified life coach. Most people know him as an everyday man with an extraordinary message that is transforming lives one at a time. The message from his story exudes "No Condition is Permanent." It's all about embracing variation, reinvention, and determination all while renewing one's mind.

BROKEN

Made in the USA
Middletown, DE
18 September 2021

48517655R00090